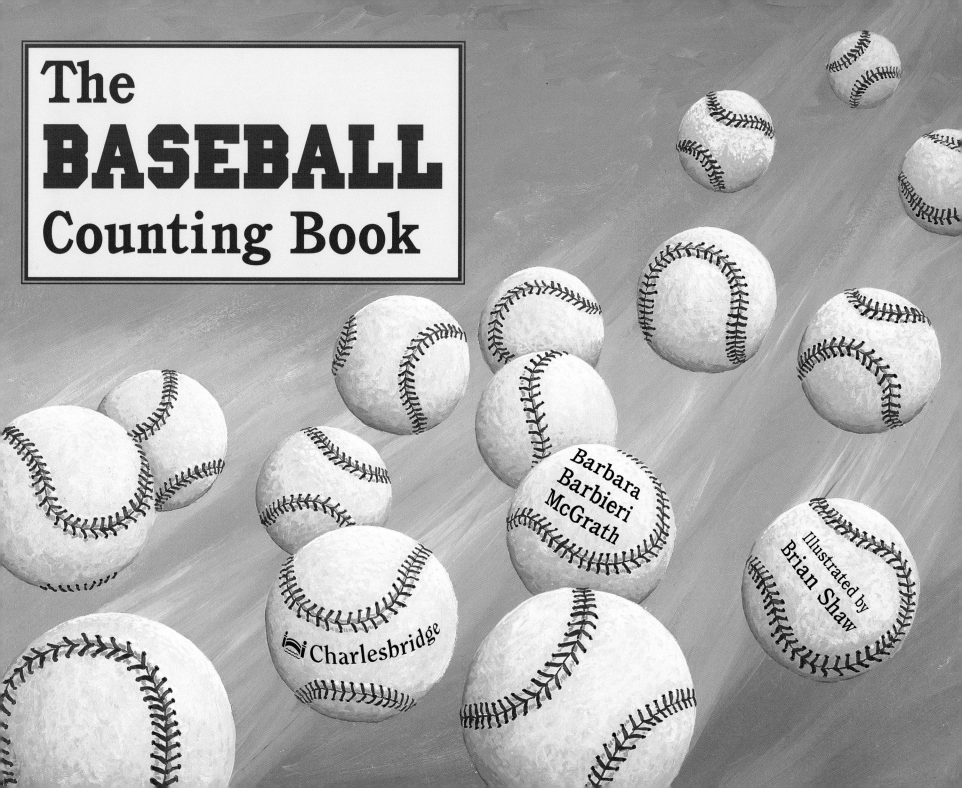

The BASEBALL Counting Book

Barbara Barbieri McGrath

Illustrated by Brian Shaw

Charlesbridge

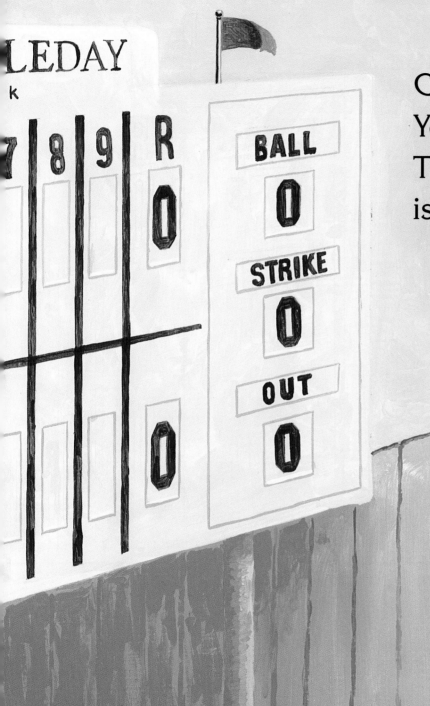

Come play baseball.
You could be a hero.
The game's starting score
is zero to zero.

0

 There will be one ball, one bat, and one call.
The game will begin when you hear "Play ball!"

We need two teams to play in the game.
Each team will have its own special name.

2

Swing and miss three times,
and the umpire will shout,

"Strike one,
strike two,
strike three,
and you're out!"

3

If the pitch is outside,
inside, high or low,
"Ball four!" is the call,
and to first base you go!

5 When there's a full count, we say, "Three and two."
Five fingers up! His turn's almost through.

Coach has a plan to tell those who are near.
The six on the infield are the ones who will hear.

6

Seven innings have passed. It's time to stretch.

These seven fans had some hot dogs to fetch!

7

The catcher has found
the one catcher's mitt.
Eight gloves are left.
Find yours. Does it fit?

Out on the field are nine places to stand.

Check to be sure each position is manned.

9

Hold the bat tightly
so that it won't slip.
Ten fingers are helpful
for the right grip.

10

11

Eleven bats to choose from—
find one that feels right.
Keep your eye on the ball,
and hit with all your might.

Here are twelve pieces of gear.
(Count the pairs as just one.)
What would you need
to get your job done?

13

Thirteen good-luck charms
make some players feel
That they will be safe
when they try to steal.

ABNER DOUBLEDAY
Baseball Park

There are fourteen letters
in this famous man's name.
It is said it was he who
invented the game.

14

15 A scorecard's one way a team's score can be seen. The scoreboard now shows the teams tied at fifteen.

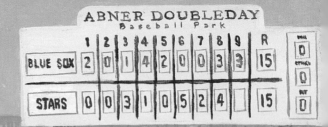

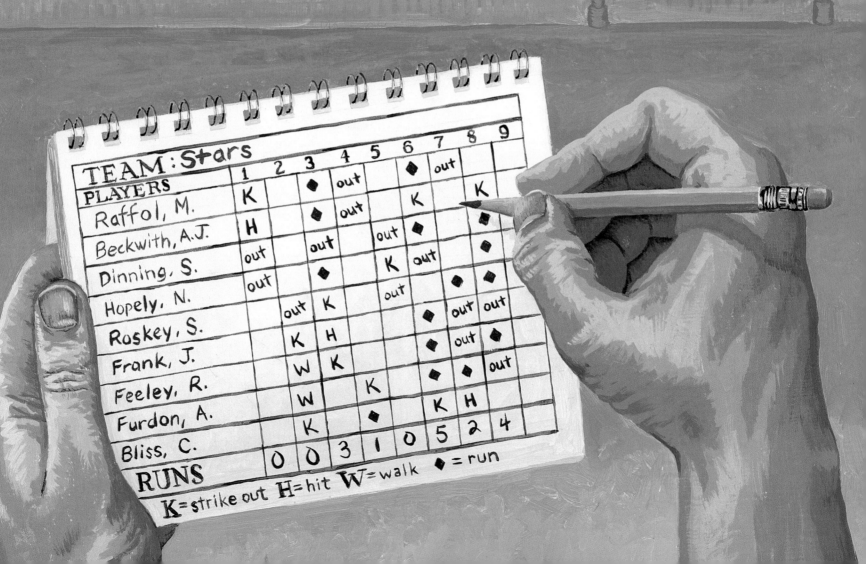

It's the bottom of the ninth,
and the pitcher will throw
Sixteen practice balls
as fast as they'll go.

16

The bases are loaded. The excitement is great.

	1	2	3	4	5	6	7	8	9	R
BLUE SOX	2	0	1	4	2	0	0	3	3	15
STARS	0	0	3	1	0	5	2	4		15

Seventeen pairs of eyes watch the boy at home plate.

17

18 Eighteen anxious players will soon hear the news.

Nine players will win. Nine players will lose.

It's a grand slam! The game is over, but wait—

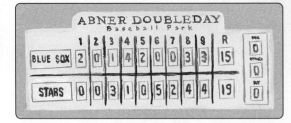

ABNER DOUBLEDAY
Baseball Park

	1	2	3	4	5	6	7	8	9	R
BLUE SOX	2	0	1	4	2	0	0	3	3	15
STARS	0	0	3	1	0	5	2	4	4	19

TOTAL	0
OTHER	0
OUT	0

Here are nineteen ice-cream cones. Let's celebrate!

19

If you love to play baseball and practice it, too,

BASEBALL CARD

strike: A strike can be made in three ways: (1) the batter swings at a pitch and misses, (2) the batter hits the ball out of bounds (a foul ball), or (3) the pitch crosses the plate between the batter's chest and knees (the strike zone). Three strikes make an out.

BASEBALL CARD

umpire: the person who makes sure the rules of the game are followed. The umpire calls the balls, strikes, and outs.

safe: what a player is when he or she gets to a base without getting an out.

stealing: running during a pitch in order to advance to the next base without the batter hitting the ball.

BASEBALL CARD

ball: a baseball, pitched outside the strike zone, at which the batter doesn't swing. If the pitcher throws four balls, the batter walks to first base.

run: a point scored when a player safely makes it around the three bases and crosses home plate.

BASEBALL CARD

out: An out can be made in four ways: (1) the batter gets three strikes, (2) the batted ball is caught in the air, (3) the ball is thrown to a player at a base before the batter arrives there, or (4) a runner is touched by a player with the ball when the runner is not on base.

grand slam: a home run when the bases are loaded. A grand slam scores four runs for the team at bat.

20

positions: The *pitcher* is on the pitcher's mound, the *catcher* is behind home plate, the *first baseman* covers first base, the *second baseman* covers second base, the *third baseman* covers third base, the *shortstop* plays between second and third base, the *left fielder* plays behind the shortstop, the *center fielder* plays the middle of the outfield, and the *right fielder* plays the right of the outfield.

Abner Doubleday: the American army officer who is generally given credit for inventing baseball in 1839. However, many historians now believe that baseball existed much earlier than this. Baseball was probably based on games called rounders and cricket that were played in England.

full count: the term for when the batter has two strikes and three balls. At the next pitch, the batter will either strike out or get on base. If the batter hits a foul ball, the pitcher will continue to throw until a strike, a ball, or a hit occurs.

bases loaded: the term for when each of the three bases has a player from the batting team on it.

inning: the period of a game when both teams have had a turn at bat. Each turn at bat is marked by three outs. There are nine innings in a regulation baseball game, although T-ball game and Little League games often have fewer innings.

One of these twenty cards might picture you!

Published by Charlesbridge
85 Main Street, Watertown, MA 02472
(617) 926-0329
www.charlesbridge.com

Library of Congress Cataloging-in-Publication Data
McGrath, Barbara Barbieri, 1954—
     The baseball counting book/by Barbara Barbieri
McGrath; illustrated by Brian Shaw.
            p.   cm.
Summary: Uses the numbers from one to twenty to
introduce various aspects of the game of baseball.
     ISBN-13: 978-0-88106-332-5 (reinforced for library use)
     ISBN-10: 0-88106-332-0 (reinforced for library use)
     ISBN-13: 978-0-88106-333-2 (softcover)
     ISBN-10: 0-88106-333-9 (softcover)
1. Counting—Juvenile literature. 2. Baseball—Juvenile
literature. [1. Baseball. 2. Counting.] I. Shaw, Brian,
1968— ill. II. Title.
QA113.M39368   1999
513.2'11—dc21   97-36610
[E]

Printed in Korea
(hc) 10 9 8 7 6 5 4 3
(sc) 10 9 8 7 6

The illustrations in this book were done in acrylic
on Masonite board.
The display type and text type were set in Cushing,
Ivy League, and Korinna.
Color separations were made by H&S Graphics, Inc.,
Rolling Meadows, Illinois.
Printed and bound by Sung In Printing, South Korea
Production supervision by Brian G. Walker
Designed by Diane M. Earley

Original photo by Chris Raffol. Digitally enhanced by Frank Mazzola, Jr.

To the undefeated Blue Jays of Natick, Massachusetts:
Patrick Walsh, Spencer Palmgren, Sam Dinning,
Robbie Feeley, Chris Bliss, W. Louis McGrath, Ben Park,
Adam Reeves, Alex Furdon, Shane Roskey,
Nathan Hopley, Matt Raffol, A. J. Beckwith, Jake Frank,
Coach Frank, Coach Raffol, and Coach Hopley

My special thanks to the extra-innings crew:
Will, E. and L., Jerry P., Brian S., Mike M.,
Juliana M., Yolanda L., Pam and Jim R., and Gini L.

— B. B. M.

To Lisa, Meghan, and Evan

— B. S.